How to
Find Joy in
Five Minutes
a Day

Inspiring Ideas to Boost
Your Mood Every Day

JOANNE MALLON

HOW TO FIND JOY IN FIVE MINUTES A DAY

Copyright © Summersdale Publishers Ltd, 2022

An Hachette UK Company
www.hachette.co.uk

Vie Books, an imprint of Summersdale Publishers Ltd
Part of Octopus Publishing Group Limited
Carmelite House
50 Victoria Embankment
LONDON
EC4Y 0DZ
UK

www.summersdale.com

Printed and bound in China

ISBN: 978-1-80007-156-8

Substantial discounts on bulk quantities of Summersdale books are available to corporations, professional associations and other organizations. For details contact general enquiries: telephone: +44 (0) 1243 771107 or email: enquiries@summersdale.com.

Contents

Introduction

Joy is all around you. It's in the little moments that make life worth living; the sparks that light you up and leave you feeling good to be alive. Joy is an energy, and scientists have found that charging your life up with it boosts your immune system, helps to fight stress and may even help you live longer.

This book takes you through a day in your life, and includes more than 60 tips and ideas to help you add joy. These simple tips will lift your mood, liven up your routine and improve your physical and mental health. Try them in any order that works for you; perhaps start at the point in your day that seems most in need of a boost. Do just one or try a whole lot — it's up to you. These tips are all designed to slot into your life easily and take no more than 5 minutes.

Start with a tip that makes you smile. Something that excites you is always easier to begin and more likely to stick. Try it out for a few days. Perhaps it'll turn into a permanent habit, or become a springboard into an idea of your own. Whatever you do, do something. Take action. Grab joy. Tomorrow you'll be glad you did.

Tell me, what is it you
plan to do with your one
wild and precious life?

MARY OLIVER

CHAPTER ONE

Happy Mornings

As you wake up to a fresh new morning, also wake up to the happiness in your life. There's so much potential for good things throughout your day. Look for the little moments of joy, hold them close and feel them grow.

First thing in the morning may be the busiest time of your day, but that makes it all the more important to look after yourself now. You can't give to the world unless you've given to yourself first. Start the day by fuelling yourself with joy and you will go further in the direction you choose.

Set a
positive intention

Before your day gets going, sit quietly and focus on how you would like to experience it. Get excited to be alive and cherish this new blank page. A world of potential is here for you as you wake up.

What positive intention will you choose for today? Where will you find delight? Your positive intention could be to notice five good things about the day, or to enjoy your food mindfully, to practise an act of kindness or to tune in to your intuition. What are you going to commit to today?

EVERY ACTION YOU
TAKE IS A VOTE FOR
THE TYPE OF PERSON
YOU WISH TO BECOME.

JAMES CLEAR

Make your bed

Making your bed in the morning is an easy way to start the day with a sense of positivity and accomplishment. It's also the first step toward good sleep hygiene and ensuring that you sleep better that night. Plump up the pillows, smooth out the covers and take pride in a simple but important job well done.

Experts believe making your bed can be an indication that you're on your way to greater things, since it sets you up in a success mindset. It's a positive place from which to begin your day: you can do this one good thing, so you can go on to do others too.

Have a (quick) cold shower

Cold showers have been credited with many physical and mental health benefits, including raised endorphins (the happiness hormone), increased metabolism, better circulation and an improved immune system — what better way to set you up for a positive day? If a fully cold shower is too much to contemplate, try standing under the water as it warms up. You'll still get a mini blast of coldness, but it'll be fleeting enough to be bearable.

Watch the sunrise

To find new perspective on life, get up early and delight in the sunrise. The start of the morning is a magical time of renewal. No matter what happened yesterday, the world continues to turn and the sun still comes up every day.

Watch how the colours change as the sun's rays light up the Earth. Tune in to the peacefulness in the air as the sleeping world starts to wake. What can you hear? What does this new day smell like? What's different about today? Be fully in the moment of the new dawn breaking, recharging yourself with peace and calm.

Write down your dreams

Writing in a journal when you wake can be a great way to clear your mind for the day ahead. Many great songs and stories started life as dreams, so this could also be a way to engage with your innate creativity.

Keep a journal by your bed and grab it as soon as you wake up, writing down any dreams you remember. What do they tell you about yourself today? What has your mind been processing while you were asleep? Dream journaling will help to clear your thoughts and give your mind added clarity for the day ahead.

Each moment is
an opportunity to
make a fresh start.

PEMA CHÖDRÖN

Inhale calm with a "box breath"

Deep breathing is a useful tool to help reduce stress and start your day feeling calm and relaxed. Here's a breathing technique to try on your commute, after breakfast or even when you're still in bed. You could also use this any time you feel anxious, or before you go into a stressful situation.

"Box breathing", also known as "square breathing" or *sama vritti pranayama*, is a breathing method that's often used as part of yoga practice. It's very simple — breathe in deeply through your nose for a count of four; hold the breath for another count of four; then exhale for four again; and pause for a final count of four. As you go through these four stages, imagine tracing out the four sides of a square (a flat "box" shape) with your breath. Repeat your series of slow breaths and pauses all around the box until you feel calm, centred and ready for the day.

You're under no
obligation to be the
same person you were
five minutes ago.

ALAN WATTS

Do a joy audit

Write a list of five things that bring you joy in life. Then think about when you last did each of those things. If it wasn't recently, then this is a sign that you need to prioritize your own needs more. Make a plan to do at least one thing from your list within the next week and put it in your diary as a reminder.

Ditch the doomscrolling

If you've got into the habit of scrolling through social media on your phone first thing in the morning, you'll know that the constant stream of news and updates is rarely positive. Some smartphones will allow you to block certain apps at times you choose, so you could try avoiding social media altogether in the early morning. Decide on a time when you're going to check your phone — maybe at lunchtime or on your commute. It's best to avoid early mornings and just before bed.

Instead, create a more upbeat plan for your morning. Get an alarm clock so you're not reliant on your phone to wake you up. Don't charge your phone right next to your bed or, if you really can't be parted from it, make sure you look at something more uplifting when you first wake up – such as Positive News, the Good News Network, or your favourite uplifting Pinterest board. Once you've ditched the doomscrolling habit, you might choose to spend that time doing something more nourishing and positive – perhaps stretching, reading, meditating or going out for a run.

Straighten up and smile

Posture can have a big influence on how we feel: cognitive scientists have found a direct connection between looking down and feeling down. On the flip side, if your body starts to act more confidently and joyfully then your mind will do so too. As you get ready for the day, straighten up, pull your shoulders back and smile. By straightening up and walking tall you'll naturally start to feel more positive. Pull your core in to support your body, smile and walk out into the world like you're happy to be here.

There is power and
strength in optimism.

SALENA GODDEN

Decide to say "yes"

We can find joy via the things we do, but we can also attract it via the attitude we take. A key element of attracting more joy into our lives is being mentally open to it. How would your life be different today if you set out in a positive direction and said "yes" to more — if you said "yes" to life? What kind of opportunities would you find yourself presented with? Who would you meet? Where would you go? Resolve to be open to possibility. See what saying "yes" attracts into your life today.

Move while the kettle boils

Exercise is one of the easiest ways to get your feel-good hormones moving, but it doesn't take a full workout to reap the benefits. Every little bit of activity makes a difference. If you like to have a hot drink in the morning, how about using the time when you're waiting for the kettle to boil to add a little movement into your day? You could dance, march on the spot, do press-ups — whatever makes it fun. If you like lifting weights, maybe keep a pair of dumb-bells in the kitchen so you can knock out some bicep curls while your morning coffee brews.

Work your wardrobe

Experts reckon we only wear 20 per cent of our wardrobes 80 per cent of the time. What hidden gems in your closet have you forgotten about? Start your day from a place of creativity and play by finding something joyful in your wardrobe to wear. Who would you like to be today?

Life is too short not to wear the red shoes; the jazzy accessory; the silk shirt. Be bright and colourful in your choices (yellow, the colour of sunshine, is often associated with joy). Perhaps you'll rediscover an old favourite in your shoes or accessories. Dress yourself with love and mindfulness rather than throwing on the same thing you wore yesterday. Every day we have the choice to reinvent ourselves by simply choosing to do something new, so have fun with this opportunity to play.

ONE MUST SAY
"YES" TO LIFE, AND
EMBRACE IT WHEREVER
IT IS FOUND.

JAMES BALDWIN

Pay yourself a compliment – and mean it

We are so often our own harshest critics. What would life be like if you were to become your biggest fan? This isn't an excuse to be arrogant. It's more of an invitation to shore up your self-esteem and recognize your own inner light when it's shining.

Look yourself in the eye in the mirror. What do you like about yourself this morning? Gaze directly at yourself and say the first kind thing that comes to mind, out loud. You could say "Well done on…", "You're great at…" or simply "I'm strong today." Pause and recognize the glow that was there all along.

Have a mood-boosting superfood smoothie

Treating yourself to a nutritious smoothie is a great way to fire up your morning and get a head start on your healthy five a day. Smoothie ingredients that are shown to boost your mood include: bananas (which are high in vitamin B6, which helps synthesize feel-good neurotransmitters like dopamine and serotonin), oats (for fibre and iron to stabilize your blood sugar levels and improve your mood) and berries (which have been credited with lowering the risk of depression). Whizz them up together with water, juice, milk or a milk alternative. See how many superfoods you can pack into your delicious daily mix.

With the new day
comes new strength
and new thoughts.

ELEANOR ROOSEVELT

Go outside and get grounded

If you've been indoors since you woke up, make a point of taking a morning break outside. If you're lucky you might be able to enjoy a cup of tea in the sunshine, but even if the weather's bad it's still worth going outside. Take time away from technology to contemplate what is going on in the world around you.

Put your hand on the ground and connect with its stillness and vibrancy. The earth beneath you is a symbol of the stability and strength with which you face the day. Use this as a reminder that you are here, now, perfect and alive, and exactly where you need to be. Pay attention to how it feels as you walk around this morning. Feel yourself being supported as you walk, stand, sit or lie down.

When you're outside, engage with each of your senses in turn. What can you see, smell, touch, hear and taste? Reconnecting with your senses will ground you in the present moment and is a great antidote to those troublesome thieves of joy: overthinking and anxiety.

Right now I urge
you in your breath,
in your eyes, in your
consciousness, invest in
the importance of this
moment and cherish it.

CHADWICK BOSEMAN

Accept yourself

The moment when we decide to do something is just as powerful as when we actually do it. With that in mind, why not decide to make today the day that you truly begin to accept yourself? Start by saying it out loud now: "I accept myself."

Think about how your day would be lifted if you were at peace with yourself; if you were happy with all you have to bring to the world today. Yesterday has prepared you for today, but your past doesn't define you. Be kind to yourself and know you already have the strength and courage to face whatever today brings.

Clear your
dumping ground

Every home has a dumping ground — that depressing, messy table top or corner where all the junk mail, broken bits and things that don't have a home gather. Pick out whatever you want to keep from the messiest area and put it in its proper home. The rest can go. Quickly, joyfully, sweep away whatever needs dumping. Put into a neat stack anything that doesn't have a place to go. If there's something that you can deal with quickly, such as paying a bill, do it straight away. Then tomorrow, even if detritus starts to drift back, it will be much easier to keep clear.

Minimize
morning stress

Becoming more alert to morning stress is the first step in eliminating it. Where does your morning flow come unstuck? What distracts you and makes it harder to get going?

One way to put some positive vibes into your morning flow is to limit the number of decisions you need to make. Streamlining your routine will make it easier for you to get up and get ready for the day. You could lay out your outfit the night before or have the same breakfast every day. Keep it simple and straightforward as you step into the day with a smile on your face.

CHAPTER TWO

Happy Days

In this chapter we're finding places to pep up your daytime and ignite your routine with joyous energy. Whether you spend your day at home, work or college, adding joy will help you get more out of your time and have fun in the process.

Your current routine didn't emerge as it is now, fully formed, and it's unrealistic to expect it to radically transform in one fell swoop. But we can do the little things: the 5-minute shake-ups that give us new perspective. As you read through this chapter, choose the bonus ingredient you'll add and do it today.

Revisit your happy place

Close your eyes and think about the things in life that make you happy. Take your mind back to your happy place and smile, then open your eyes and bring that smile into your day today. Your happy place may be an actual place, or it could be a book, film or TV show you enjoy. Even if you're not doing those activities right now, you can still take yourself there in your mind and relive the benefits. Going to your happy place is like taking your mind on holiday.

Who you are today...
that's who you are.
Be brave. Be amazing.
Be worthy. Be heard.

SHONDA RHIMES

Say three thank yous

Pausing to say thank you is a great way to appreciate the good in your life and spread that feeling out to others. Studies have found that grateful people feel healthier and experience fewer aches and pains. Another study found that grateful people even sleep better and have reduced stress and better mental resilience.

Don't take life or people for granted. Think of three things in your life that you're grateful for right now. Name them as you say thank you for them. If they involve another person, perhaps you could send them a thank-you note or message; let others know that you appreciate them.

Gratitude opens the door to more relationships and deepens existing ones. What will your three thank yous be for today?

GIVE TIME, GIVE
SPACE TO SPROUT YOUR
POTENTIAL. AWAKEN
THE BEAUTY OF YOUR
HEART – THE BEAUTY
OF YOUR SPIRIT.

AMIT RAY

Have a healthy mid-afternoon snack

Look for joy and colour in the food you put into your body today. Planning a healthy snack will help to naturally eliminate unhealthy snacking while also giving you a mid-afternoon energy boost.

Nuts and dried fruit are a great pick-me-up and are packed with nutrients. How about a banana, some berries, oats (in the form of a flapjack or porridge), an orange for vitamin C and fibre, or a boiled egg or Greek yoghurt for protein? Have fun planning a really delicious and appealing snack to treat yourself to in the afternoon.

Consider the clouds

We miss so much of the world by not looking up, particularly the ephemeral wonder of clouds. Allow your mind to wander as you look up and notice the shapes carved out by the contrast of white and blue. What's going on up there? What are the stories in the shapes?

Perhaps you could go the scientific route and find out what some of those cloud shapes mean. Can you tell your nimbus from your cumulus? Enjoy your cloud gazing, whether it's a learning opportunity, a creative prompt or simply a time to sit back and pause in your day.

You are
powerful
and your
voice matters.

KAMALA HARRIS

Take a break

Sitting in the same place all day isn't great for the body, so no matter how busy your day, make sure you take regular breaks to move around. Don't just slide from one task to the next. Make a point of getting up and away from your workspace regularly. You'll work more effectively when you take a break to consider what you've just done and prepare yourself for what comes next. Wearing a fitness monitor will remind you to take some steps every hour, or if you don't have one, simply make sure that you get up from your desk and stretch after every phone call, email or meeting.

Carry out small acts of kindness

Research suggests that little kindnesses sprinkled throughout your day will give you a boost of oxytocin (the love hormone) and dopamine – this is why we feel good when we're kind. It's a chemical reaction. Psychologists have also found that the joy of giving lasts longer than the joy of getting, so if you give to others you will actually feel happier in a more sustained way than if you were simply to consume more. Actively look for ways that you can be kind today, whether it's holding the door open for the person behind you in a shop, picking up litter or donating to charity.

Get social

Break up your working day by chatting to someone in person – perhaps a co-worker, a friend or the staff at your local sandwich shop. Social interaction (even if it's just chatting about the mundanities of your day) will give your mind a much-needed break. It'll help you focus on the wider world and get you through the mid-afternoon slump in a more positive mood.

Whether you work alone or as part of a team, interpersonal relationships are part of what makes life worth living. But they don't always flow naturally, and sometimes you will have to work at them and put the time in to help them flourish. So, take a few minutes out of your day to phone or message a friend, have a coffee date with a colleague or check in with someone you haven't heard from in a while. If you can't connect with them today, get something in the diary to look forward to. Your connections will grow stronger and be more supportive the more you nurture them. Think of your personal and professional relationships as being another part of your well-being that needs to be taken care of, just like any other mental or physical needs.

It is not joy that
makes us grateful;
it is gratitude that
makes us joyful.

DAVID STEINDL-RAST

Enjoy a
hand massage

If you spend a lot of the day doing manual work or using a keyboard, your hands and wrists will be working hard. Take care of them and treat them with love. They are your most precious work tools, after all.

Pause to grip and flex your hands. If you have a little hand cream nearby, use it to help soften the skin. Massage each knuckle in turn, and all around each cuticle bed. Doing this will reduce your stress and anxiety levels, release any muscle tension and increase hand strength, and will be a little spot of luxury amid a busy day.

Choose something new at lunchtime

Joy can often be found when we stretch our comfort zones and try out something new. One simple way to do this is by choosing something different for lunch. What sort of cuisine haven't you tried before? Is there a new local cafe that you haven't visited yet? What kind of leftovers are lurking in your fridge, ready to become something new?

Little adjustments like this shake up our sense of who we are on a very basic level. Challenge your assumptions – perhaps who you are has changed without you noticing; maybe you *do* like mushrooms now. Try one new thing in your lunch today and expand your horizons.

What today will be
like is up to you.

STEVE MARABOLI

Go for a
walk outside

Taking a few minutes to head outside into the sunshine can make you more productive, so try this to give yourself an energy boost for the last blast of your working day. Exposing yourself to sunlight tells your body it's time to be awake and alert, as the daytime sun sends an activating energy boost to the clock in your brain. This will then help you sleep better when it's dark at night.

Sunshine also boosts serotonin levels, so an outdoor stroll will also improve your mood, and help you stay calm and focused for the rest of the day. Plus, it'll give you a daily vitamin D fix (essential for your immune system and for keeping your bones, teeth and muscles healthy). In short, there's not much that a bit of fresh air and sunshine won't help!

INSTEAD OF WORRYING ABOUT WHAT YOU CANNOT CONTROL, SHIFT YOUR ENERGY TO WHAT YOU CAN CREATE.

ROY T. BENNETT

Prepare for tomorrow

Take 5 minutes to clear your desk at the end of the working day. Write a list of the things you need to do the next morning. Put things back where they should be and dump any waste in the bin. This sends a strong signal to yourself that it's the end of the working day. Imagine how joyful it'll feel to sit down at that clear desk tomorrow. It's like giving a present to your future self.

What you want out of tomorrow could be emotional as well as material. What do you want your watchword for tomorrow to be? Write it down where you'll see it first thing.

Treat yourself

Add in a tiny luxury to your day. Pause to smell a beautiful flower; apply a spritz of your favourite scent; choose the fancy brand of tea for your morning drink. Even taking 5 minutes to pause in your busy day can feel like a luxury. Finish work 5 minutes early today and chalk it up as a gift to yourself. What have you done today that is for you and you alone? What could you do? What does luxury mean to you?

Make contact

Physical touch creates a sense of closeness and comfort. Not only does it help reduce stress, but it promotes the healing process too by reducing levels of cortisol — a hormone that can weaken the immune system. Incorporate some physical contact with another living being into your day, whether that's hugging a friend, stroking a pet or holding a loved one's hand. Remember that everyone has different levels of touch that they are comfortable with, so keep it consensual and ask permission if you're unsure if it will be welcome.

Get rid of joy-suckers

The objects we surround ourselves with can have an incredibly powerful effect on our state of mind. Look around at the place you spend most of your day. Do the things around you lift you up or make your heart sink? If it's the latter, why are you keeping them in your life? Get rid of three things in your environment that drag you down – put them in the bin if they're unsalvageable, or consider donating them if they might offer joy to someone else. Removing them will be an instant boost to your joy level.

A joy-filled home
is like your own
personal art museum.

MARIE KONDO

Pause for zazen

Zazen is another word for sitting meditation. It's done sitting upright, to help us pay attention to the body and the present moment. The aim is to become more balanced and centred.

Sit quietly and breathe — maybe using the box-breath method from page 16. Your mind is likely to jump all over the place with crowds of thoughts, but be led by your still body and regular breathing. The calm will come if you wait for it.

There is no wrong way to do *zazen*. All you have to do is sit and breathe, and be at peace with yourself. Traditionally this is done for the length of time it takes an incense stick to burn, but start with 5 minutes and see how you get on. Frequency is more important than duration with meditation, so even 1 minute every day is better than 30 minutes once a week.

Go on a joy walk

The more you look for joy, the more you will find it, so put on your rose-tinted glasses and go out into the world with the aim of noticing things that will lift your heart. Where are the colourful parts of your environment that catch your eye? Which shapes are shifting in the sky today? What kind of people do you notice in the neighbourhood? Any cute dogs being walked today? (We could all learn a lot from the enthusiasm of dogs.) Seek joy wherever you find it and honour it by holding it in your heart.

Mark the transition from work to home life

Mark the end of your working day and close the door on it, either literally or metaphorically. It's easier to do this if you work outside your home because your commute will provide a natural break and a chance to switch from one mode to another.

If you work from home, try incorporating a joyful daily ritual that signals the end of your working day. You could light a candle, or sit somewhere new (not your workspace) to have a quiet cup of your favourite beverage. Step away from your workday stress and toward the freedom of the evening.

CHAPTER THREE

Happy Evenings

The evening may be the part of the day when you have the most choice about how you spend your time, but it's often a period when energy is on the wane. Injecting a little joy will give your evenings an energy boost so that you savour them rather than collapse into them.

As you wind down, consider the hours just gone and prepare for the next day to come. The tips in this chapter will help you make the most of your evening as you reflect, recharge and prepare for tomorrow.

Learn from today

Every day has the potential to teach us something if we let it. Step away from any sense of guilt over whatever didn't go right today. Instead, pause and ask yourself, what was good about today? And what will I do differently tomorrow? What did I learn today that I can use in the future? If you like to journal, write down three things you learned during your day. Gather the gifts that the day has given you and carry them like treasure into tomorrow.

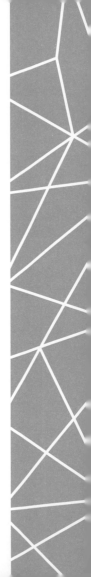

The art of being happy
lies in the power of
extracting happiness
from common things.

HENRY WARD BEECHER

Forever is
composed of nows.

EMILY DICKINSON

Enjoy quick spa time

Take care of your body to honour and appreciate the fact that it has carried you safely through another 24 hours. If your feet are tired after your busy day, you could soak them in hot water or rub in some scented moisturizer. Or you could apply a quick face or hair mask as you settle down for the evening. Thoroughly cleanse and exfoliate your face, removing the built-up grime of the day. Help your skin feel refreshed overnight and show that you are grateful for all it has done for you today.

Make room for 5 minutes of creative play

We've all seen how joyful children get when they're lost in play and there's no reason why adults can't access this state too. Let your creativity loose and have some fun. Get out a notebook or journal and spend 5 minutes drawing a self-portrait, making handprint paintings or writing a letter. No one is ever going to see this but you (unless you want them to), so feel free to express yourself.

You may enjoy colouring or crafting, going outside to run through leaves or jump in a puddle, dancing to your favourite tune or decorating a cake. Play is more about the process than the outcome — your picture doesn't have to be perfect and your cake needn't be dinner-party worthy. The journey is the reward. Have fun playing and see what you can create.

Take a photo every day

Mark the passing of time with a daily photo that sums up the joyful moments in your day. You might want to snap it on your daily walk, when you wake up or when you get home in the evening. Some apps are great for this, letting you build up a picture of your life with a daily photo or video. Celebrate the everyday good stuff by capturing it as it happens. When you look back at the end of each month you'll see the richness of your life in action.

IF WE DID ALL THE
THINGS WE ARE
CAPABLE OF DOING,
WE WOULD LITERALLY
ASTOUND OURSELVES.

THOMAS EDISON

Make easy overnight oats

Overnight oats make a delicious, nutritious no-cook breakfast and can be easily prepared in under a minute the night before. When you're pottering around the kitchen or making your evening meal, put around 40 g (½ cup) of oats into your breakfast bowl. Add around the same amount of milk (or milk alternative). Throw in a few berries, or a spoonful of yoghurt or seeds — whatever you like. The milk will soak into the oats overnight, leaving a delicious pudding-like texture. Put the bowl in the fridge until the morning, ready to enjoy.

Dance in the
ad breaks

Dancing has been credited with being great for mental and physical health. It improves your posture and flexibility, and it's an easy way to lift your mood. If you're watching television or YouTube videos in the evening, add a little fun activity by dancing in the ad breaks. Even if you're feeling tired after a busy day, this is a quick way to enjoy the benefits of movement without leaving home.

Give yourself a hug

Hugs are incredibly comforting and a huge help in feeling safe, loved and secure. If you're apart from your loved ones, you can still engage with the power of hugs by yourself. This movement is often used as a stretch as part of a yoga routine, but there's no reason why you can't do it at any time.

As you clasp your arms around yourself, feel the stretch across your back and through your shoulders. If you've spent the day at a desk or hunched over a keyboard, your muscles and spine will thank you for this move. Use it as a way to comfort and acknowledge yourself and everything good you did today.

You got through today and that is worth celebrating. You are worth celebrating. So, wrap both arms around yourself and give yourself a hug.

Think of all
the beauty still
left around you
and be happy.

ANNE FRANK

Eat your evening meal outside (yes, even in winter)

Try something new for your night-time routine by eating your evening meal outside. If it's cold, just wrap up warm — you won't be out there long; you can do it! If the stars are out, see which ones you can identify, or maybe there'll still be birdsong in the air. Leave your phone inside as you enjoy your al fresco dinner. Take a quiet, tech-free break to enjoy a relaxing meal.

Stand on one leg

This is a simple, fun way to work on your health from the comfort of your own bathroom. Balance is a key component of fitness and is also linked to good brain health. To see how yours is doing, stand on one leg as you brush your teeth tonight. This helps develop better balance, engages the core and strengthens the legs. Swap legs halfway through so the benefits are evenly spread. It's always easier to add in a new habit next to something you already do, so linking this to your tooth-brushing time is a way to ensure that it happens regularly.

The little things?
The little moments?
They aren't little.

JON KABAT-ZINN

Set up a sleep-friendly bedroom

Spend 5 minutes before bedtime making your bedroom more sleep-friendly. Start by moving your laundry out of sight by gathering it all into a basket. If the room is cluttered, you don't have to sort things out at this stage — put them in a box or a bag for now. Get the clutter out of the way quickly so the space feels clearer. Maybe you won't miss all that stuff. Maybe you didn't need it after all.

In particular, put any electronic devices out of sight. Your bedroom is not the best place to charge your phone — in fact it's probably the worst place. Dim the lights. Spray some perfume in the air or light a scented candle. Put a book you love by your bedside, to encourage you to read a few pages before you go to sleep. Lay out your favourite nightwear and get ready to relax.

Make a date
with laughter

Laughing is one of the most purely joyful activities we can do. It's fun, free and so easily accessible. Nothing will lift you up like a good belly laugh. Include something funny in your evening routine – perhaps a podcast while you're doing the dishes, half an hour of a beloved TV show or checking in with your funniest friend. As well as relieving stress, laughing will stimulate your organs, boost your immune system and improve your mood. Time spent laughing is always a joy.

Find 5 minutes of unplugged quiet

Step away from any screens and take some quiet time to recharge at the end of your working day. Notice the natural ambient sounds of your home – the people, the house creaks, the cars going past outside. Focus on the sound of your own breath. Reflect on whatever or whoever brought you joy today – when did you smile? Recalling it will mean you smile again and relive the joy twice. Enjoy these 5 minutes of peace and positivity as your day winds down.

Life isn't meant to be
lived perfectly... but merely
to be LIVED. Boldly, wildly,
beautifully, uncertainly,
imperfectly, magically LIVED.

MANDY HALE

Light a candle

A lit candle can be a lovely way to add ambience to your evening. Perhaps you could light your candle mindfully in memory or in celebration of someone. Perhaps you'll do it in celebration of you and your victory in navigating another day. Who lights up your life right now? It could be someone you know or someone you admire. Light a candle for them and be thankful that they are in your life.

Read one positive page a day

Perhaps you've been intending to read more, but never get around to it or haven't got the focus for it at night. Reading one page a day is where it starts. You could choose to start with a poem, short story, or a book that's more pictures than words.

It could even be an essay, a Wikipedia page on a topic that interests you or a positive news article online. If you enjoy it and it lifts you up rather than brings you down, then it's worth doing.

One page that you read slowly and carefully may have more impact than a whole book you struggled through and forgot about. Even short bursts of reading like this can help you improve your mental focus, feel more positive and learn something new, as well as nourishing your mind.

Play classical music before bed

Studies have shown that listening to classical music lowers body temperature and heart rate, and calms breathing: ideal for inducing a restful night's sleep and helping end your day on a blissful high. Put some classical music on in the background as you get ready for bed. You don't have to be able to interpret it or have any knowledge of the music at all — just go with the emotion it evokes in you. Let the music take you to a calmer, more joyfully uplifted place. And if classical isn't your thing, white noise or rain sounds can also provide a calming aural backdrop.

You look ridiculous if you dance. You look ridiculous if you don't dance. So, you might as well dance.

GERTRUDE STEIN

Schedule something to look forward to tomorrow

Studies show that anticipation can actually be *more* enjoyable than experiencing the thing you're looking forward to. Remember how Christmas Eve as a kid was often more fun than Christmas Day? It will actually make you happier today if you have something to look forward to tomorrow. Get your diary out and see what's coming up, or where you could slot in something fun. Maybe message a friend or book a ticket to set it up. Once you've decided on something you'd love to do, put it in your diary and feel the glow of excitement grow.

CHAPTER FOUR

Happily Ever After

So far we've looked at short-term bursts of joy; little things you can do quickly to help your here and now become happier. Given how much joy can lift us up, how can we incorporate more of it in our lives and feel those benefits in a lasting way?

The suggestions in this final chapter might take a little longer to do, but they'll set you up for a future mood boost whenever you want it. We're making those little sparks of joy a priority, so they combine into a fire of true, pure meaning, fulfilment and happiness. Make your joy habit permanent and feel the benefits rippling out into your future.

Survey your strengths

Focusing on your strengths will help you feel more confident in all areas of your life. And boosted confidence will lift up your days, adding joy wherever you need it. So turn your attention to the good stuff.

What are you good at, both inside and outside the workplace? Where have you excelled in the past? How do these strengths show up in your life — what have you done with them? What would you like to do with them? Write down at least five strengths you've shown recently.

Choose a soundtrack for your life

Music has been proven to have a powerful effect on the brain. Listening to music you loved when you were younger can give your memory a boost as you reconnect with the feelings and emotions you associate with those tunes.

Think about the kind of mood you'd like your playlist to evoke — which may not necessarily be the mood you're feeling now. Would you like to feel calmer? Or more energetic and motivated? Curate a playlist with that in mind and take joy in the activity of doing so. Then in the future when you want to access those feelings, you've got the unique soundtrack already created for it. Perhaps you want something to keep you moving on your morning run, or to enhance your confidence when you're feeling under pressure. This is a gift to the you that is yet to come — give a treat to your tomorrow self by creating your soundtrack now.

I don't think that loving yourself is a choice. I think that it's a decision that has to be made for survival.

LIZZO

Sort out your socks and underwear

The small tasks can be so satisfying! Pair up your socks. Toss away any that don't have a mate. Then your underwear — weed out anything that's got holes or doesn't support you any more. Watch a few folding videos on YouTube to find a way of storing them neatly in your underwear drawer. Fold, roll and arrange them in an aesthetically pleasing way that makes you smile. Take pleasure in the process — then every day when you open your underwear drawer, you'll instantly access that joy again.

Forgive someone

This is a simple but challenging task that can go very deep. It's important to let go of the past so that we can move on into a better future. Clear the path of past hurts, mistakes and regrets and you are on your way to freedom.

Who will you forgive today? Perhaps there's more than one person. Picture them in your mind and say out loud, "I forgive you." If you can't find it in your mind to forgive, what would it take? How can you let go and be happy to be free?

Sail away from the
safe harbour. Catch the
trade winds in your sails.
Explore. Dream. Discover.

SARAH FRANCES BROWN

Focus on
your future joy

This is a follow-on from the joy audit on page 19. Write down at least 20 things that you think might bring you joy in the future; little things, from ice cream with sprinkles to an unexpected rainbow or a hug with a friend. There is no right or wrong to this — each person's list will be very different and you're not going to show it to anybody.

Then write down at least ten things that have brought you joy in recent days. Cast your mind back over the past few weeks and remember when you found yourself smiling, or were boosted in a positive way.

How do the two lists compare? Are the things you think might make you joyful the same as the things that actually do? Is there anything from your "might" list that you could easily do today (get that ice cream)? Are there any themes emerging? Where does joy come from most often in your life and how will you get more of it?

Reconnect to your passion

What did you once enjoy doing that has fallen out of your life? Did you love to paint, read, write, listen to music or play a sport? Reconnecting to this forgotten passion will bring added meaning to your life and ignite you with energy. Passion equals enthusiasm and connects with our inner well of deep joy. Start in a simple way by using your free time to work out how you might get going again with your passion. Gather any resources you need and write down in your calendar when you're going to start.

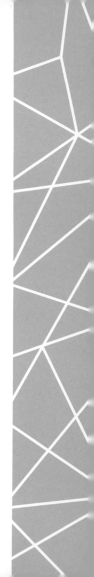

Focus on what you're good at

If you're considering a career change, it can be hard to know where to start. Why not start with looking at where the joy is in your current working life? What skills do you have — what things can you do that make you or others happy? Write down ten things you're good at. The mix of these skills are the ingredients in your own personal recipe for success. Which training or educational courses have you completed? Do any of them need updating? What are the most called-for skills in your industry (or the industry you'd like to move into) right now?

Make a "let go" list

Write down things you want to let go of in your life. It could be a negative habit or relationship, or perhaps an unkind way you treat yourself. It could be things that have served you once but are not serving you now. What are you ready to let go of in order to feel more open to future happiness? What would make you happy not to have to think about or be ground down by again? Write them down on a piece of paper and then throw it away. Letting go physically will ready you to let go emotionally.

Great things are not done by impulse, but by a series of small things brought together.

GEORGE ELIOT

JOY IS TO FUN
WHAT THE DEEP SEA
IS TO A PUDDLE.
IT'S A FEELING INSIDE
THAT CAN HARDLY
BE CONTAINED.

TERRY PRATCHETT

Plan a trip

Where have you always wanted to go? What places would you be disappointed *not* to have seen before your next landmark birthday? Take out your most beautiful notebook and plan your dream trip.

How will you budget for it? What will you do when you get there? You could create a mood board with inspirational pictures of the place you want to go, or draw a map and work out your dream itinerary. With small steps your dream can become reality.

Jump for joy

For such a simple activity, the benefits of jumping are immense. Jumping can build strength and bone density, as well as improve your metabolism and heart health. The endorphins produced will help you feel relaxed and improve your immune system. Moving like this naturally increases your dopamine levels, meaning that you're guaranteed to feel good even after a brief workout — perhaps that's why they call it jumping for joy!

Start your jumping routine twice a week and build up to five days out of seven. Do as many as you can in 5 minutes — or more if you feel like it. Try it while watching television or playing music. Choose from:

♦ **Jumping jacks** — Spring out then back in again for a little cardio to warm up the muscles.

♦ **Jump on a trampoline** — It's kinder on the knees than jumping on the floor. Use either a mini indoor rebounder or an outdoor model if you have access to one.

♦ **Jump squats** — Squat down low then leap up to the sky.

Create a
self-care basket

Make it easier to look after your skin by gathering together a self-care basket of goodies. This could include a nail file, some hand cream, nail polish remover, moisturizer or cleanser. The easier you make it to treat yourself with kindness, the more likely you are to do it — particularly if you've had a bad day and need a pick-me-up. Make taking care of yourself fun rather than a chore.

He who kisses
the joy as it flies
Lives in
eternity's sunrise.

WILLIAM BLAKE

The drive toward joy is the drive toward life.

———————————

INGRID FETELL LEE

Connect with inspiring people

Use social media to connect with new, positive people, and curate your feed so that the people you follow lift you up rather than drag you down. If you appreciate what someone has brought to your life, you can spread the joy further by telling them. You'll both be glad you did. This could be someone you already know, or an artist, writer or musician whose work you find inspirational. Reach out to them and let them know how their work has had a positive impact on you.

Pick up litter

This is a really practical way to make a difference to your day-to-day environment. Spend 5 minutes picking up and disposing of the litter on your street. You'll probably want to wear gloves and maybe use tongs to pick things up. Do it joyfully, focusing on the fact that you are enhancing the beauty of your surroundings. Care about the world around you. Be a passionate cheerleader for it. Studies have shown that places with less litter attract less litter, so this will have a far-reaching effect.

Adopt a piece of nature

The world is full of miracles just waiting to be noticed and enjoyed. Open your eyes to the natural beauty all around you. Today, take time to see your surroundings in more detail, especially the parts of your neighbourhood that you pass every day but have never stopped to consider.

Perhaps you could mentally adopt a tree in your local park, or a plant in your neighbour's garden. Notice its journey as it changes with the seasons, from first buds in spring, to bloom, then bare again in winter. Be in the moment and connect to the beauty of the natural world.

Appreciate yourself today and tomorrow

As we lay the foundations for future joy, it's important to stay connected with the present and appreciate who you are now, today. Charging up your own sense of self-worth in the present moment is one of the best gifts you can give yourself for future benefit.

Write down three good things about being the age you are now. What do you know now that you didn't know ten years ago? What have the most challenging parts of your life so far taught you? What are you glad that you don't have to think about any more? Perhaps you've put exams or school pressure behind you. Maybe you have more freedom now than you did when you were younger and can make your own choices rather than having your life controlled by others. Maybe you're more comfortable in your own skin now; more at peace with who you are. Appreciate everything that's good about you, here, today, now, forever.

Let us make our future now,
and let us make our dreams
tomorrow's reality.

MALALA YOUSAFZAI

TODAY WAS GOOD.
TODAY WAS FUN.
TOMORROW IS
ANOTHER ONE.

DR SEUSS

Conclusion

As we've seen throughout this book, the wonderful thing about joy is that it's very easy to find. It isn't hiding or locked away. You just have to reach out and touch it. Whatever's happening in your life, there will always be something little you can do to attract more joy. And when you do, the benefits to your physical and mental health will be immense.

Now that you've got plenty of ideas for how to find joy, it's time to take action. What are you going to do? Which was your favourite out of the ideas in this book? Commit to joy. Aim to do at least one joyful thing every day. That's where you'll really make a difference in your life. And by filling yourself with joy, your positivity will spill out and touch the lives of those around you. The world will become a more joyful place just by having you in it. Think of it — a world with more joy and you at the heart of it all.

Five minutes, that's all it takes. Take a step; take a leap; take action. Embrace joy. Embrace life.

Have you enjoyed this book?
If so, find us on Facebook at
Summersdale Publishers, on Twitter
at @Summersdale and on Instagram
at @summersdalebooks and get in
touch. We'd love to hear from you!

www.summersdale.com